TIME TO KILL SPARROWS

TIME TO KILL SPARROWS

*A Kaleidoscope of Verse by Diplomats
and their Families*

Editor: Peter Hinchcliffe

Illustrated by Lynne Price

In support of
Action on Disability and Development
CARE International UK
Children in Distress

The Book Guild Ltd
Sussex, England

The Book Guild Ltd,
25 High Street,
Lewes, Sussex

First published 1999
© Peter Hinchcliffe 1999

Set in Bembo
Typesetting by Raven Typesetters, Chester
Printed in Great Britain by
Antony Rowe Ltd, Chippenham, Wiltshire

A catalogue record for this book is
available from the British Library

ISBN 1 85776 398 X

CONTENTS

FOREWORD

(By The Rt Hon. Lord Hurd of Westwell, CH, CBE)

So now I know what they were doing, as they gazed out of the aircraft window, scribbled at meetings where there was no need for a record, or walked in solitude up and down the Ambassador's lawn. They were writing poetry and this is the admirable result.

Poetry is the result not of idleness but of a life so charged with feelings that they have to overflow. A diplomatic life, whether for diplomats or their families, has particular characteristics which shine through their poems. They include the wandering, the arrivals and departures, the packing and unpacking of household goods. They cover the contrast between abroad and home, particularly home after retirement,

> spat out at sixty
> a stranger in a country you thought you represented.

But Peter Hinchcliffe wisely decides that in the end he is going to enjoy life, even after sixty. There must be room in a diplomatic life for wit, for example in the famous theological parody by Sir Hughe Knatchbull-Hugessen, 'Quicunque Balt', reproduced here. Also for nostalgic contrasts between past and present in a foreign country, as when Mina Dresser celebrates moonlight in a Suzhou garden, and contrasts it in the next poem with the revolutionary Peking task of killing sparrows. And for calm sad beauty, as with Angela Greenhill,

> Bliss is an empty room, a curtain glowing
> Yellow on the sunlight, in the seawind blowing;

Congratulations to all those who contributed to putting this collection together. May it encourage others to be bold, and channel their ideas and emotions into the most demanding and worthwhile of all forms of expression.

Douglas Hurd

EDITOR'S INTRODUCTION

From what I saw during my time in the Diplomatic Service it is evident that there are many individuals skilled at a great variety of art forms not usually associated with civil servants. This anthology celebrates the diplomatic poets. 'Poetry' in this case including light-hearted office doggerel as well as more serious verse. The authors are by no means all serving or former diplomats. A narrow majority of the contributors are spouses and I have included two very young authors – aged 9 and 11 when they wrote their verses – to represent that part of the Foreign Service family which one of my daughters used to call 'diplobrats'. Some of the poems have been published before, either in the in-house magazine produced by the Spouses' Association or in poetry magazines or in individual anthologies.

I am delighted that Lord Hurd agreed to write a foreword. I asked him not out of any discourtesy to New Labour and the present team of Foreign Office Ministers. He was a very popular and respected Foreign Secretary and in addition he is a writer (albeit not of poems) and above all a former serving career diplomat. He seemed the obvious choice.

Apart from the sheer pleasure of putting together this anthology I also have a more serious purpose: to raise money for three organisations working in the Third World. Action on Disability and Development (ADD), CARE International (UK) and CINDI (Children in Distress) in Kitwe, Zambia, all have Diplomatic Service connections. ADD and CARE have co-operated with the FCO in a number of projects in developing countries. (Heads of Mission in some countries can draw on funds for small-scale developmental projects in a programme known as the British Partnership Scheme – often working with non-governmental organisations and drawing on the expertise of the Department For International Development.) The contribution to CINDI is in memory of Cecily Eastwood, whose poems appear in this volume and who was tragically killed in Zambia in 1996 whilst working as a part-time volunteer with CINDI during her 'gap' year. A fund has been set up to help continue the work with which she was involved.

Some of the verse may not be 'deathless' in the classic sense. But I hope that, at least, it will be enjoyable.

Peter Hinchcliffe

THE CHARITIES

Three charities or development organisations will benefit from profits made by the anthology:

CARE INTERNATIONAL UK

CARE International UK is the British member of a ten-country family of charities that together form one of the largest emergency relief and development aid organisations in the world.

CARE aims through its international structure to avoid wasteful duplication in the delivery of aid, to achieve economies of scale and to operate on a scale which makes a real difference. It works in partnership with local people in the poorer parts of the world (63 countries in Africa, Asia, Latin America and Central Europe) to enable them to improve their economic and social status. Besides being active in the traditional fields of development – improving people's access to food, water, sanitation and health care, and providing support for small businesses – CARE has developed expertise in the provision of 'non-traditional' forms of aid, for example mine-clearance in Angola and trauma counselling in Bosnia.

In 1998 CARE International UK helped fund projects in 43 countries. CARE's operations as a whole reached nearly 25 million of the world's poorest people.

ADD (ACTION ON DISABILITY AND DEVELOPMENT)

ADD is the only British-based development agency supporting development work exclusively with groups of disabled people in Africa and Asia (13 countries in 1998). On the basis of 12 years' experience, ADD is well placed to support disabled people's organisations as they work to persuade governments and development agencies to adopt policies inclusive of disabled people. Disabled people are their own most powerful advocates. ADD helps them gain the skills they need to become effective campaigners, to take control of their own lives through self-help initiatives to raise their standard of living and to build up their confidence in their own worth, abilities and rights.

CINDI (CHILDREN IN DISTRESS) KITWE

CINDI was established in Lusaka, Zambia, in 1989 with the aim of supporting orphans within their communities. It is under the auspices of the Family Health Trust, an umbrella organisation for NGOs working to counter AIDS or alleviate its effects. CINDI Kitwe (a town in Zambia's copper belt) is an autonomous branch of the Lusaka-based organisation with 9,000 orphans registered with it. It provides counselling, food and help towards school fees, textbooks, uniforms etc. It encourages and empowers local communities to look after their orphans. Basil and Alison Eastwood (he is British Ambassador in Damascus) have set up a support fund for CINDI in memory of their late daughter Cecily to continue the work she did in Kitwe with CINDI before her death in Zambia in June 1997.

CYNTHIA BARLOW MARRS

Cynthia Barlow Marrs (Mrs Tony Gooch), an American by birth, is an environmental planner with a visual arts background. She left the US in 1984 to work in South Africa, where her first published poems appeared in The Poetry Workshop 1987, *an anthology which arose from working sessions led by Professor Ridley Beeton at the University of South Africa. Having met and married her husband Tony Gooch, then serving in the British Embassy in Pretoria, she has continued her career through subsequent postings in the UK, Poland and now Singapore, where Tony is Deputy High Commissioner.*

Hesperus

When I sleep, it is in the gesture of your arms,
warm inside knitted fleece which has known
your body well.

When only breathing moves the dark
and dream glimmers on the edge,
ghost-curve of your back fits the bend of my spine,

mending spent desires and half-wrought wishes
into peace.

Sending dreams like ribbons flung into space
to catch your sphere,
I sense the shadow of your voice soft upon my neck,

your calm hand lambent upon my head,
your voice speaking
the language of dreams.

Sleuth

I could scale your high-security walls
after dark
and wander incognito between the pine trees
and the secrets there;

unnoticed
amongst the unspeakable dreams
the soft edges of the aching past
the sharp outline of your great ambitions.

I could pry the clasp of your romantic impulse
under a quiet moon
and spill the contents winging like wild moths
under your astonished eye;

or try the heavy lock on your hidden human nature,
and with the gentlest probing fingers
test the temper
of your finely honed defences.

I could be your shadow
and thereby escape scrutiny.
I could penetrate what you think is protected,
do no harm,

and leave you with the ache of knowing
that it had been done
and that you did not
die.

Faux Pas

He said he loved my feet.
I looked at them in wonder, surprised
at the treasure under me.

Ten flushed indignant moons
glared back, unblinking.
We, they said silently,

tread on air for you,
put our best selves forward for you.
My mutest apologies

I said, hoping to change the subject
(he was praising the sheen of my hair).
Ten very pink small voices said:

Be glad
that your feet make your head
light.

Retreat

Who littered desire in this empty room,
the bed with a question for its quilt
soft and yielding;

Whose voice spoke and moved invisibly away?
I might be where I shouldn't be,
might leave this place lonely as before:

The corners weep for company,
small sounds creep restlessly across the floor;
repentance sleeps in the crack under my door.

Effects

At the little moat we all laughed –
the white silk parachute on the grass,
wicker hampers overflowing.
It was August, an African Spring.
We had champagne.

We were our fizzy, polished best.
In conversational pleasure boats we rowed,
ocean wide, across the grass
lightly gliding out and back again.

Our laughter carried like tinkling glass,
we were magnanimous as mist on a lake.
Corks popped like parachute ribbons,
our little wit-flotillas steaming in their wake,
tiny tête-à-tête propellers churning.

You and I left the others
small and soundless on the shore,
our oars, our voices, dipped and rose
streaming.

Giving

These gifts are given to us:
A measure of space, some time, a little light
    The sense of being
    The grace to breathe.
Leave the petals where they fall.

All this we know: there is no transience,
Nothing passes. Everything, every act
    Is significant
    Between what we are taught
And what, by degrees, we learn.

Nothing disappears –
The light merely changes;
    We adjust and shift our focus,
    And when it moves
We slowly focus again.

How luminous these petals,
How recurrent their fall –
    Herein lies the seed
    Herein curls the snail;
Above, the swallow dives

Below, the spider comes home;
Little lives live here.
    All of this, and we are unaware:
    Everything, all of our life, began
With such very small gifts.

DERRICK BEAUMONT

Before his retirement in the 1980s, Derrick Beaumont served in Cyprus, Sierra Leone and France. He has now, as he puts it, 'come alive in Spain', where he and his wife live. Writing poetry is a hobby. Of his three poems, one, 'Ego and Essence', has appeared in the FCO's spouses' journal.

Ego and Essence

('What if all we see and seem is but a dream
within a dream?' *Edgar Allan Poe*)

Then self is an illusion, just a dream
Though in our poor confusion it may seem
The central point round which the stars rotate
And worthy of divine concern its fate.

From this 'firm base' the universe we scan
To study nature's laws and know God's plan.
Examined in the mirror of the mind
Meaning and truth and purpose are defined.

But it's no magic mirror that we bear
And everything we see reflected there
Distorts to fit our egocentric view
Which, when we wake, will disappear like dew.

Pass through the glass and nothing more shall be
And all that ever was has never been.
The dreamer wakes, the dreamer was the dream
A bubble breaks on Life's eternal stream.

Now

('But thought's the slave of life, and life time's fool;
And time, that takes survey of all the world,
Must have a stop.' *W. Shakespeare. Henry IV, Part 2*)

When, as a schoolboy, Shakespeare's rhyme
Drew my attention to the mystery-time,
My future seemed a never-ending way
My past, so brief, was with me every day.

Well here I am still living quite serene
Within this Now in which I've always been
As child and youth and ever-ageing man
The eternal Now that compasses my span.

Days gone, no longer brief, long shadows cast
Through memory's dusty window on the past
I glimpse lost loved-ones lingering as shades
As my remembrance of their history fades.

The 'never-ending way' now I can scan
My finite expectation I can plan
Yet I remain where I have always been
My ever-lasting Now still holds the scene.

When this now ends, true to life's laws
Nothing – O Bard – need give me pause
No fears, no dreams, no mystery
No how! The mystery is Now!

The Doctor's Dilemma

Unto flesh born yet unto spirit bound
Cruel and forlorn, indeed the Faustian choice.
Blind faith as monarch absolute is crowned
Reason and instinct are denied a voice.

Unlikely promise of eternity!
For this renounce the pleasures of your prime
Or, with the damned, the happy and the free
Lie with the devil in the sands of time?

LADY (MARY) BEST

Mary Best is the wife of Sir Richard Best, who retired from the Diplomatic Service in 1991 having had Iceland as their last posting. Her 'A Song of Security', written for the amusement of one of their children at boarding school, was based on experiences of having homes made secure in both Lusaka, where they were from 1969 until 1972, and Kaduna, Nigeria, from 1984 to 1988. Sadly many posts, especially in Africa, suffer from major security problems – a British diplomat was quite recently killed as the result of a mugging incident in Kenya. In many poor countries diplomatic property is regarded as fair game for often heavily armed and ruthless robbers. The theme of Mary Best's poem is that Overseas Estate Department of the FCO (responsible for the 'Diplomatic Estate' overseas) should not rely on getting a good job done locally in certain countries.

A Song of Security
(Or the other side of diplomatic life)
(With apologies – mostly – to Flanders and Swann)

'Twas on a Monday morning the welding man arrived,
To fit us up with burglar bars, on our french-windows side;
They tried to match the welding points but they just didn't meet,
So we sent them off to make some more – and they came back next
      week.

Oh! It all makes work for the welding men to do.

'Twas on next Tuesday morning the welders came once more,
With blow torch and acetylene to fit them to the door;
They started joining up the bars but they didn't fit again,
So we ordered them to take them off and not come back again.

Oh! It all etc.

'Twas on the Wednesday morning the Boss Man came to see
The awful work the welders did and he said 'Most sorree
I'll get them back to put them right, so don't you fret no more';
So they are coming back tomorrow, just to even up the score.

Oh! It all etc.

'Twas on a Thursday morning they started yet again,
With cross pieces that fitted and bars to take the strain;
The painter covered the blistered bits with white paint in a stream
And we had to work the rest of the day to get the parquet clean.

Oh! It all etc.

'Twas on a Friday morning those welders came once more,
To put some extra solid bolts upon our landing door;
We covered up the furniture, the carpet and the floor,
But the hot bits found their way right through, and left us feeling
      sore.

Oh! It all etc.

'Twas on a Saturday morning, the painter came again,
I hope he makes a better job, I'm weary with the strain;
I've made a vow that I'll not break, no workmen here for me,
Until I've had my mid-tour leave and restored my sanity.

Oh! It all etc.

'Twas on a Sunday morning, oh bliss! No workmen here,
I look around, the bars are sound, the paint seems to adhere.
I hope the message has got through, to our friends in OED
That it's better to send a welder out – than do it locally.

ANNE CLAY

Anne Clay has accompanied her husband Edward on a number of postings including Nairobi, Sofia, Budapest and Nicosia. Edward's last overseas job was High Commissioner to Uganda from 1993 to 1997. Her two poems, both written in Kampala, will touch a chord with most members of the Diplomatic Service. Whatever the popular perception of diplomatic life may be, certain aspects, especially the socialising, dull the mind, drench the liver and most of us would love to dispense with them.

Cocktail Lament

Always be cheerful and kind, darling
And keep up a ready wit
Never confess you're upset, darling
Remember, you're always a Brit.

So what if the carpets are muddy
With guests standing back to the wall?
Pretend all the world is your buddy
And move a few out to the hall.

The servants have drunk all the gin, dear
No problem, there's plenty of wine.
Keep serving the pizza and dips, dear,
Be thankful they are not here to dine.

Half past eight was the time they were leaving
But now it's half nine and they're here.
Broken glasses? Don't waste your time grieving,
They've just finished twelve crates of beer.

Appearance must be maintained, darling
It's vital to work all the while.
The Office is proud of you too, darling.
So bite on the bullet and smile.

Diplomatic Departure

I am stepping off the roundabout
No more shall be for me
The Cocktail and the Luncheon round
The Dinner and the Tea.

I am taking off my uniform
And hanging up my plumes
Goodbye to pearls and calling cards
And fine, exotic blooms.

Forget about the social round
Don't call me; I am not there.
The chit-chat of the drawing room
Will vanish in thin air.

Farewell to gloves and dazzling smiles
To canapés and wine
For Blighty calls as darkness falls
On the receiving line.

The 8.15 shall carry me
Through suburbs closed and grey
And Sainsbury's shall be my lot
And washing-up each day.

So greetings anonymity
While I am still in my prime.
The life abroad and all its joys
Shall cease; until next time.

KATHY CLAYDEN

Kathy Clayden is currently in Lagos, where her husband Timothy is working in the British High Commission. She comes from an expatriate background and even before she set foot outside the UK had a passion for maps and to 'live abroad'. Before joining the Diplomatic Service she was an academic doing research and tutoring undergraduates. Her first posting was Warsaw. She has written stories as well as poems and has entered national and international competitions. She was awarded 'Highly Commended' in the Richmond and Kingston competition and Second Prize in Envoi *magazine's International Poetry Competition. The Nigerian flavour is strong in some of these poems.*

Seeing over Aisles

Tall I stand, tall.
Not strong nor athletic falling over in flats
pavements saying hello,
but tall I stand.

I see down supermarket alleys,
count the number of heads bobbing
like apples on a surface of hair.

Tall I stand. Tall as I was –
'thin and lanky', 'chicken legs' –
careful to avoid cracks
stepping over drains
I grew like a seedling in the dark.

Tall bones creak
one on top, one below
or rotate, round and round
smooth and polished.

Lying flat they dissolve like years;
photographed, recorded, scanned,
their decay remembered in numbered futures
more accurate than Gypsy Lee
who looks for length as long as I am tall.
Doesn't see that predictions like bones
can make you fall.

Louisa

When we met again you gave me Allium
– three of them
their heads a haze of purple
a halo round a core, like your daughter's hair.

I clung to you
afraid
you'd melt back into daydream.

I arranged the flowers in a vase, cut them so they staggered,
gave them direction, north, east, west.
Each day their dandelion-clock faces beamed
as I met them on the stairs
counting the days.

Best Price

'Sister, sister', 'foreigner'. Fingering
their wares they seductively call,
smoothly stroking long soft fabric, unrolling it
whistling as you walk past. 'Best price'.
Sometimes they touch you with one finger, gently.

Stopping brings shouts from owners
and young boys emerge, unwinding
themselves like bales of cloth from the darkness.
Showing interest forces helpers
to tumble
colours of blue, green, red
over arms, floors, propped Pisa-like.
The man in the next concrete booth leans over
tempting with yellow.

Trapped, the bargaining begins,
in ritual dance, fabric under fingers – his first price, a joke.
Laughing you offer him starvation
and he wails clutching at cloth his 'last price'
unfurled between you.
Another offer, he shakes his head and states 'best last'.
You cringe, stumble away
and trip the gauntlet of trader's deputations.

He follows
fondling, fussing and folding out streams of cloth,
binds you to your compromise.

Knots of men and boys unravel
rolling themselves back onto stalls.
He flicks the notes like a fan, frowning.
Hand in pocket he turns, soliciting 'last price, sister'
as you weave your way unmolested.

Sandwiches and Pop

With balsa swords and sunburnt legs,
we spent the days in killing pirates
bodies flotsam on the beach
each echoed surge our battle cry.
Farewell holidays in Torquay,
where shells from rock pools dripping
salty tears sang tales of pounding waves.
Of ships on rocks that danced
and kicked the smugglers' tune
and waves that broke, and broke again
against a timbered carcass.
The grinding white hard surf that left
some shattered, splintered matchsticks
and cries of floundering seamen caught,
like bees in honey, drowned by winds
that stormed and danced in blood.
Great sails tugged free of tangled lines
and ripped in push-me-pull-you games
all thrown, left in tattered pieces,
confetti strewn beyond the tide.

A A O   OP IN   EN RE

It should read FALAMO SHOPPING CENTRE
in fluorescent letters three feet tall.
Instead the 'S' dropped, squawking like a Parrot.

Held in slipping bondage a man reaches
to possess pendulous red clumps
oozing with oil. Next door Palm as wine
drip drips into discarded plastic
empty as the beggar girl's stomach
on Third Mainland Bridge.
The 'M' got smashed she mumbles.

In the middle of traffic, a man
with shopping bagged trousers tightens
string knots, pulls down a crisp 'P' packet hat
passes the blind man with his child guide
knocking out a 'T' on car windows.

The 'L' falls. Lines off the bridge
flung into a creek,
floating effluent and corpses bathed daily by the sea.
Question mark fish hoisted higher
and higher, then picked off like scabs.

The taxi's 'H' hop in potholes. The Kombi's
sides shaking like jelly stuffed with
strawberry ripe, plum burnt flesh
advertise, 'Jesus washes me of my sins'.
Both clank clank in front or stop. 'G'
grinding to a halt. Armoured vehicles
with money or expats race gun toting past.

'C' Comfort on the corner, 30p to spread legs.
Too tired from standing,
sits on the ground misses the punter.
Lipstick kisses on windscreens, smeared
then cleaned everyday by 'F' Freedom,
(and like the Shopping Centre)
a name he will never grow into,
but overtime he earns driving Master
may bring passing comfort to him.

LADY (MAVIS) COULSON

Lady Coulson accompanied her husband, the late Sir John Coulson, to Paris, New York and to Stockholm, where he was Ambassador. They later had seven years in Geneva during John Coulson's time as Secretary General of EFTA (European Free Trade Association). In 1980 Mavis Coulson published a book of poems, Turning Wheel, *under her pen-name of Ninette Beazley. Her other publication is* Southwards to Geneva, *a book on early English travellers to Geneva. Her poem on 'Shock' will bring back memories to those of us who have been remorselessly dragooned into helping to organise charity events — an all too often inescapable commitment, especially for senior (female) spouses in many posts.*

Madonna: Wild Cherry

You lean, and cradle all that was, and is.
The lily-time of waiting's over. Now
In flame and amber you fan out
Protective arms. Insidious winds
Of winter blow your gown. As each
Bronze pendant dreamily descends,
Awareness of *Pietà* grows,
Engulfs . . . till from the mulchy floor
Below, there's stirring . . . All the Heart
Of Immortality is there. . .

Magnolia Grandiflora

'Tout passe . . .'

And was it only yesterday
You shouted joy, and dazzlingly
Unfolded Easter cups
In white abandon? How
Could one night of searing frost do
This – transforming radiance into
Holocaust of brown and withered parcels?
No, this may not, cannot be the end. We
Turn for comfort to the cyclic round. 'Next
May', you say . . . Next May? But that is twelve unknown
Months ahead. It's *now,* oh stricken tree, we
Crave your loveliness!

28

Shock

I am not here. The Village Christmas Fair
Is shuffling to a climax. 'Ah, you're there!';
The Vicar shouts – and sprints towards Denise,
The Raffle-Lady. 'Vicar, hurry, *please*'
She squawks: 'High time we drew . . . what's that you say?
The bottle-stall's collapsed? . . .' Oh no, I am not here.

I am not, am not here. Instead I tread
A petalled rug, while jacarandas spread
Blue, blossom-flaunting branches towards the sky;
And tiny crowing girls are swinging high.
'. . . So can you help? Three dozen sausage-rolls . . .
That's all we need!' No, no! I am not here.

I am not here. The little bush-fringed lake
At earliest light is tranquil. As we wake,
Mt Kenya's snow-draped peaks are mirrored deep –
And coots process in duplicate to keep
Their morning tryst . . . 'Yes dear, a sponsored slim!
Just sign this form!' No, no! I am not here.

I am not here. I am where fish-eagles scream
Their wildness on Naivasha's shores. There's gleam
Of lake in ancient lava hills; and by
Tall reeds at dusk the grunting hippos ply
A battered track towards home. No, no! You choke
Me with your worthiness! I am THERE – not HERE!

Summer Airs

This sodden spring, the chill
Of Genghis Khan possessed
Our valley. Sap
Moved sleepily.
No bird
Was heard.

Now May is nudging June;
And once again the stream
Goes chortling through
Dark hollows, layered
In green . . .
Unseen.

And suddenly, the thrush
Arpeggios . . . and brims,
And overspills
In wildest joy
Above
You, love.

While higher up the stream
The willow-wren outpours
Its offering from
Another world –
Unknown,
Yet known.

31

LIZ COX

Liz Cox and her husband are nearing retirement, having served in Pakistan, South Africa and Europe. She is an English teacher, which profession she has generally managed to practise during her husband's overseas postings. She therefore has what personnel people in the FCO refer to as a 'portable' career – not always the case with diplomatic spouses. She has written for the South African History Review.

The Crunch

Now that we eat at home alone,
No noisy flow of talk from eldest son,
No scornful silences from two to heed,
No sauce or salted butter, oft forgot
To bring to tempt the palate of our youngest one.
I find we munch and crunch,
We smack and chew
Our cereal and crispy lettuce leaves
And high baked Jacobs scarce to be endured.
And soup, ah soup, what torture is that slurp?!
And talk, desultory flow of trains and rain
Does not stop up the noise but merely helps
The sticky smack, the squelchy crunch.
Quite privately I do not think it's me.
But when accused the father of the three
Offended turns and with defiant munch
Declares he misses them as much as me.

RICHARD DAVIES

*Richard Davies, born in 1942, has recently left the
Diplomatic Service. He served in Hong Kong,
Cyprus and Thailand. He now divides his time
between the UK and a farmhouse in France, which he
and his wife have restored. He has been writing poetry
as a hobby in order to interpret the world around him
and in the hope that his poems 'will bring pleasure as
well as insight to those who read them'. 'Swans' is
my favourite.*

Swans

Where once sea flowed
and sowed
the marsh's salt seeds
a vast company of swans,
for all the world like
white, white sheep,
ebbs and flows
beside the reed-banked dykes.
Sheep close by
watch them graze
and gaze at them with sad eyes,
as they leave
to seek a water pasture new.
They watch them spread their wings
to launch
their awesome progress in the sky,
fifty strong,
silent but for the sawing of great wings
in the clear winter air.

As their eyes behold
the parting birds,
do the sheep
wish their dreams could have wings
and that they, too,
could soar
white-pinioned in the air?

Buskers – Covent Garden

Buskers in the Piazza
do all the things
I was not allowed to do
as a child.
They play with fire, and shout and
throw balls high in the air and
dance and sing and whistle and
make girls squeal
by dragging them out of the crowd
to make fools of them.
They do all these things watched by
people like me
who still have childish urges
to misbehave in public.

Moving I – 2 December 1996

It will not be the moving but the leaving
that will make us sad.
We shall close the door
on a part of our life,
and when we press our ears
to its weathered wood
we'll hear the echoes
of all the music and laughter,
the sounds of our hopes and our fears
the faintest traces of the whispers and the shouts,
that have filled this house for a dozen years.
Outside we'll press our faces
to the window's lozenged glass
and glimpse the fleeting shadows
the light and shade of memories
which live on, ghosts in the wainscot,
part of the fabric of the house.
We shall shed a tear or two.

It will not be the moving
but the leaving that will make us sad.

Moving II – 2 December 1996

We did it!
We turned our world upside down,
packed it into a box
and moved.
The familiar shibboleths,
the household goods
of pictures, prints and books,
we threw, haphazard, in a van
and sent them on their way.

Safely here
the mosses that have clung
to the rolling stone of our lives
confronted us, stuffed into cardboard,
and challenged us to restore them
to their former virtue.

Threatening and yet cajoling
they urged us to be bold.
Slowly they have left their wraps
and in new and different lights
they give again to walls
and shelves
the certitude and constancy
that bring ease of heart
and make, once more, a home.

Fireworks – Bourdeilles. 4 August 1996

We stood in the crowd on the bridge
to watch bright blossoms bloom
high in the dark foliage
of the evening sky.
Giant sprays of red and green and gold
that flowered and flared,
shedding petals of fire
in the night air.
From the river
sharp shooting silver stars
whirred and whizzed and banged
and lit the town with vivid lightning strokes.
As one such incandescent bud burst,
you turned to me,
your face alight with awe and pleasure
and we laughed
and held each other close
and marvelled at the artificer's art.

GREG DOREY

Greg Dorey transferred from the Ministry of Defence to the FCO in 1986, having served in the UK Delegation to NATO. He then worked in Hungary and is now a Counsellor in the British High Commission, Islamabad. Surprisingly he has never submitted his poems for publication except in his school magazine. I feel they deserve a wider audience. 'The Rise and Fall of the Tabloid Diplomat' pokes gentle fun at some media perceptions of 'Our Man' in wherever.

Ley-Lines

From Stonehenge to the Avebury rocks
Across the leys of ancient power,
Marked by the lines of rugged blocks,
Scored by the sun each passing hour.

How should it be if, with a primitive faith,
I wandered sole among the deep-carved symbols?
Saw through the gloom a distant, floating wraith,
And heard the note of flute and beat of timbals?

The mystic barrow lies overhung
By inky cloud on a grassy sward.
With echoes of a warrior's dirges sung.
And, deep within the tomb, an iron sword.

Nature's Child

Autumn leaves, falling in whorls;
Scratching the surface of slime-green pools,
While the sea mists rear up to the cold stars.
Behind the window something stirs.
Chapped lips draw back from sharpened fangs –
Mind vacant, dwells on distant things.
A spark of intellect, sharp as a glass sliver,
Crosses the face before the mouth slavers
And the moment passes.

Between the gates he goes then through the rushes,
Wading down the river towards the lights,
Then out of sight;
Enters the sewers –
Nostrils flared, savours
The night-soil scent
Bloodshot eyes scan . . .
A small rodent scurries by.
Talons grasp, incisors bite,
Hunger slaked
Its pace slackens.
Moving through the gloomy dark
Where foul things lurk.
Pushes up the manhole cover,
Through the gap it quickly slithers...
Excitement mounts, its body shudders
Then retreats into the shadows,
To watch intently. Here come tapping
Dainty feet on cobbles tripping.
Flash of lace in lamplight glistens.
First a leap and then a whimper,
Ending in a crimson bubble
And smacking joy with rapturous gurgles.

As the rush of energy flows through,
It throws back its head and howls at the moon.
Then hears footsteps running and faraway shouts,
Windows are lighted, a nearby shot . . .
Back down the manhole, retreading its route,
Feeling so strong now it fears no fate.
The fingers of dawn are gripping the river.
As the sea mists still hover.
Then down to the cellar, away from the day.
Nature's child is full of joy.

The Rise and Fall of the Tabloid Diplomat

I start at the office at ten o'clock sharp,
By half past, I am quite peckish for brunch.
I return to my room for a meeting or two,
And by noon I could do with some lunch.

If there's much work to do, then I am back there by two
(If there's no one of note at the club).
Then it's write, write, jaw, jaw, 'til a quarter to four,
Which is when I pop out to the pub.

Now's the time for a snooze, while I sleep off the booze
Until six, when receptions have started.
Then I wander around trying all of the snacks
Until most of the guests have departed.

There is just about time to change into black tie
(It's a good job I live fairly handy);
And after fine wines and a mountain of food,
I roll home with a skinful of brandy.

I'm a great fan of caviar and larks' tongues
And this is foie gras! You should try it!!
It's rather a bore. If my gut grows much more,
I shall have to consider a diet.

You may think this sounds undemanding.
But that's really unfair, I must say;
The busiest job it may not be, but
It takes up quite a chunk of one's day.

I would much rather stay here in London.
I find foreigners rather peculiar.
And so does my girlfriend from Knightsbridge,
The svelte and well-britched Lady Julia.

They've tried to teach me foreign languages –
The fact that they have failed makes me proud,
There was never a crisis which could not be solved
By my speaking in English, quite loud.

When abroad, I spend most of my time by the pool,
Playing croquet, or sipping some champers.
And I pray for respite from the hardship
(In the form of a few Harrods hampers).

But I fear that the office is changing
As accountants begin to move in.
The esprit de corps's disappearing
And it's harder to find a free gin.

What's this in my tray? A P60 you say?
Well, I don't think that's very funny.
How to fill up my time, without turning to crime?
It's a good thing I've got private money.

MINA DRESSER

Mina Dresser and her husband Clive have had a number of diplomatic postings including Venezuela, Peru, Chile, Germany and Nigeria. Peking seems to have made the greatest impression on her, as it was during their posting to China that Mina wrote the bulk of her poetry. I was especially struck by her shortest contribution – 'Time to Kill Sparrows' – from which the title of the anthology is taken. Whenever possible she has followed her singing career and has given stage, radio and TV recitals in the UK, Germany and South America, plus performing background music for several Australian films; one of which was selected for Cannes. She now teaches music.

Untitled

Her eyes are fields of pain, where sons
had toiled, coerced, compelled, till
gentle hands were bruised,
misshapen or deformed.

Black slogans, etched in deepest fold
of brain, for once lie dormant, mute, inert.

She dozes now, nods restlessly
as Gobi breezes sough.
A half forgotten joy of Shanghai youth
lights her pale face in sleep,
a flashing image in a murky pool.

She dreams of weddings, gongs, sedans
and small red slippers, satin bound
and cheong-sams flapping, open
to the waist, and silken lanterns
glowing in the dusk.

She stirs, stiff limbed and heavy eyed,
as restless ghosts, their red-nailed fingers
splayed like fragile starfish, sob
in watery graves.

A Suzhou Garden

Tender moonlight perceiving the city at midnight
pervades the silent garden to its very corners.
Soft hued saffron roses and pallid lilies slumber,
while oleanders dream and hollyhocks stand
tall, sentried, like T'ang warriors shadowed
against the darkened ochre of the crumbling walls.

Pale moonbeams, now hanging thread-like
from the dark blue sky, crinkle stone flagged paths
into guileless secrecy, and black pools
with languid willows mirror the tranquillity
of centuries past.

The aged scholar sits motionless, with silken robes
Cocooning him into soft sensuousness, while
the white crane, with jade-like beak and scarlet crown
stands close, aloof in its quiet and solitary elegance.
These two, lost in their singular world of purity and grace.

A moonbeam falls, and water ripples.
Man and bird fly heavenwards and the garden rests
in its sleeping loveliness.

Time to Kill Sparrows

Mid morning.
The sun is bright.
No clouds.
The city stops.
Tools collected
for daily task.
Saucepan, cane, pole, stick
or anything else
that is useful.
Eleven o'clock strikes.

Time to kill sparrows.

(The killing of sparrows in Peking was a revolutionary duty in the 1950s. Mass participation in pest control is no longer practised.)

Ayi

Morning starts at dead of night.
Queue to wash.
Ayi[1] shivers. Water icy.
Rodents lurk.

Bedroll folded. Baby woken.
Black eyes rubbed in faint pale light.
Ayi fondles. Milk is heated.
Guzzling. Wide contented smile.

Hutongs[2] stinking. Hutongs stirring.
Pigeons[3] fly.
Ayi battles. Wind fights water.
Murky dawn.

Crone gapes welcome. Grandchild folded
into aged withered breasts.
Ayi kisses. Tears approaching.
Lengthy journey still ahead.

No more sounds of whushing bike wheels.
Horns now blast.
Ayi struggles. Dangerous roadways.
Dirty black.

Water splashes, soaking body.
Legs dull, leaden. Face is raw.
Ayi treads wheels, ankles painful.
Hums to lighten heavy toil.

End of journey now in sight.
Treadwheel stops.
Ayi tidies. Hair in order.
Work day starts.

---

1 'Aunt'. Name given to domestic servants.
2 Chinese quadrangle housing – usually slums.
3 People on bicycles are known as 'flying pigeons' in Peking.

Life's Surplus

Everywhere the girls in desperation
huddle; unwanted. Not for them the joy
of life's air, to fill their lungs with giving gulps
of breath, clean and bright. Only numbers

above the bare shared beds give identity –
four two seven, four two eight; birthdate unknown.
Discovered – Wuhan. Thrown away – Xian.
Refuse disposal, they cling to life.

Refuse to die. A faint cry goes unheard
and no one comes. Tiny bound feet echo
in sympathy along the corridors of
forgotten decades. No hope at all

for these market economy rejects.
A little one shudders and life slips away.
No torment, ill treatment; just no loving care
and quiet neglect is all that's required.

SALLY DUMAS

Sally and Tim Dumas were with us in Jordan, where Tim, a Gunner colonel, was Defence Attaché. They are now on a similar assignment in Abu Dhabi. Sally's poem 'Arrival' records the feelings of a brand new Attaché's wife coming to terms with accompanying her husband on his first diplomatic assignment – very different from regimental duty. As for 'Another Dinner' – this no-show phenomenon by VIPs is a familiar hazard in diplomatic entertaining.

Arrival

How long has it been?
Is it only two years since that drive into town
On a hot July night,
Our life in suitcases (eighteen I recall),
All senses racing, nerves in freefall.

Long past the months of classroom grind,
Muddled, fuddled, cross-eyed, by aliffs, dots and lines.
Worn pencils, worn brain, those verbs were insane!
So briefed and briefed, it had become quite a bore,
And up to my ears in the rights and the wrongs
Of 'the Arab Way',
I was King Hussein'd out.

Then, the shock of the new as reality bites –
We've arrived!

Jebel on wadi, rolling, drained and stark,
Minarets echo in praise of Allah!
Biblical tableaux amaze and astound,
How strange it all seems – strange smells and strange sounds.
Warning bells toll!
Do I sense hostility, feel threatened
By this very difference all around?
Feeble cowardice crooks a wily, wary, finger.
Never felt like this before - *can* I, *will* I cope?

Get a grip girl!

Two years have passed, July is here again.
Sleeping cat by my side, I am content,
Part of the scenery – and it didn't take long,
My doubts and fears smothered
By the gentle innocence
Of an ancient, bygone age,

Trapped beneath shrouds and veils.
This arid beauty and faded splendour
Have enveloped me.
'Neath cool blanket of vines
I hear the soothing wail of prayers,
While gnarled, nutbrown Bedou
Shepherds his motley herd t'ward home.
I am warm and secure.

Can that have been me, that paranoid mess?
What a difference two years make ... oh yes.

Another Dinner

Another dinner tonight, we're all dressed and pressed,
Pictures straightened, silver gleaming,
Though I'm not keen, I confess.
But I've thought it all through - menu chic and tempting,
No garlic for her, no red meat for him.
It's under control, I'm feeling cool.
I'm serving Queen and country –
(I hope they like *moules!*)

This dinner of mine will be quite a big deal!
The guest list is awesome but my mission is clear,
There'll be generals and generals, even a Prince, wow!
(It'll be sheer miracle if they all appear).
Here comes another dinner, another dip affair –
'Mix me a horse's neck please, dear'.

The date was for eight (they're usually late),
But it's already nine and still no sign.
If they don't come soon we'll have prawns by the ton,
And my chateaubriand will be chateau-well-done.
Oh, the titivation and suffocation
In a scorching kitchen,
The shopping and chopping and mopping and cooking,
And those goooorgeous flowers, they took me hours!

Khalil and Adeeb wait patiently in the wings,
Salvers of drinks, friendly grins.
Telephone issues its ominous squeal,
'I'm browning my souffles . . . please get that, Khalil?'
'It's the palace, madam, to say they can't come,
Very sad, very sorry,' Khalil's looking glum.

His news isn't new but it's all too true –
NONE of them coming? HRH too?
Gazumped at the post by a bigger fish
From some Balkan state, now ain't that rich?!
I curse and I storm but I feel no pain.
It's happened before, it will happen again.
'Adeeb, Khalil, Edna, pull up a chair!
We'll feast like the gods on this fabulous fare!'

CECILY EASTWOOD

Cecily, Basil and Alison Eastwood's third daughter (he is Ambassador in Damascus), was tragically killed in a vehicle accident in Zambia in June 1997. She had been working in her 'gap' year in a school in Kitwe in Zambia's copper belt. I am including two of her poems – 'School's out!' written when she was nine (!) and the other, 'Catharsis', when she was sixteen. A memorial fund – The Cecily Eastwood Memorial Account – has been established to support the work of CINDI (Children in Distress) in Kitwe. Cecily worked there as a volunteer in her free time and I would like to make a contribution to CINDI from the proceeds of this anthology.

Catharsis

The prologue, warm and rising ebb,
The face cupped, waiting
Anticipation of the sea-salt smell, of
Their caress.
Then, tender crease, the
Eyelids drop. Heat flowing now,
Red spikedwhite tide;
And they fall,
The diamonds of release.

School's Out

It was the last lesson,
A typically hot Sudanese Friday.
I restlessly shifted around in my chair.
The teacher droned on and on
In an incessant river of French,
Which gurgled from the back of his throat.
How I wished the day was over!
At last the bell rang.
We jumped joyfully out of our chairs,
Hastily packed our school-bags,
And tore, at break-neck speed,
Down the stairs and out into the sunshine,
Breathing heavily and sweating in torrents.
Then we burst out laughing,
For, thanks to our silence,
The master had forgotten to give us any homework!
We waited impatiently for the cars
For at any minute the schoolmaster could remember.
At last my mother's battered old Suzuki came in sight,
Bouncing in the air most of the time,
With my mother at the wheel,
Steering with one hand,
And holding on to her sunglasses with the other.
I leapt into the car and said
'Quick, let's get out of here!'
My mother obeyed, and,
Just before we turned the corner,
I saw the enraged teacher
Run out of the gates waving a homework sheet.
'Phew!' I said, 'school's out!'

SIR WILLIAM GORELL BARNES

William Gorell Barnes, who died in 1987, had a distinguished career in the Home Civil Service. His appointments included personal assistant to Clement Attlee, Under-Secretary in charge of Africa in the Colonial Office and a member of the UK Delegation negotiating membership of the EEC. Earlier service in the Foreign Office included postings to Baghdad, Madrid and Lisbon. I am indebted to Lady Gorell Barnes for the following poems.

The Eternal Question

Sand has innumerable grains
Our hair has countless strands.
The reason no one explains
For no one understands.

Sand is weather-beaten rock
Ancestral apes had hair;
But these dry facts do not unlock
The door to whence and where.

Here let religion stake its claim
Seek our submissive nod:
The mystery is still the same;
For who created God?

I am Alone

Not that voluptuous sinking into solitude
Mirroring myself in shadowy pools.
But something raw like an open wound and crude
Rushing naked in a crowd of fools.
I am alone.

No cloth to staunch me and no woman's hand
To feel with frightened eye my fevered head.
Only the sun now on a sun-struck land
And the hammer of my heartbeat in my head.
I am alone.

But the play goes on and in their usual places
The players sniff the nature of my wounds
But pass them by and from their public faces
Behind the wineglass make their predestined sounds.
I am alone.

Norfolk Landscape with Figures

Fields upon fields, and lanes
going nowhere important.
Huge Constable trees, black tracery
on white, gold, green,
not sculpted by the wind
like Cornish trees,
but sturdy as an old man,
remembering
the walk to Norwich in his youth,
thirty miles there and back,
driving slow cows through the night.

Villages not huddled in a dip,
but set square round the church
where men are known and accepted
with their faults
because there is no one else.

Skies not eaten by the roll of hills
but broad skies
diminishing both life and death
within the great hoop of horizon.

THE LADY GREENHILL OF HARROW

Angela Greenhill, a former member of the Foreign Office, became a Diplomatic Service spouse during the Second World War in Cairo, when she met and married Denis Greenhill. Her husband had a very distinguished career, finishing up as Head of the Diplomatic Service. Angela is a very accomplished poet. She won the Literary Review's Grand Poetry Prize *in 1994 and has had a number of poems in the magazine. Her 'Letter to an American Artist' won the Kensington & Chelsea Arts Council Poetry Prize in 1996. She has published an anthology of her poetry:* All Things Relate. *In addition to six of her works I could not resist including 'I Wish' by her granddaughter Aster Greenhill, written when she was ten or eleven!*

Letter to an American Artist

On a clear day you saw the Pyrenees
appear as if by magic overnight
and put on canvas that skyscraping frieze,

but on an April day, perverse and chill,
could you have seen our London cherry trees
cascading into flower down Notting Hill.

I think your brush had trembled in your hand
like a live thing – what comparable thrill
to that of seeing spring invade the land?

All Brunswick Gardens like a ballet corps
of girls with tutus slightly out of hand,
exuberant blossoms, bursting buds galore,

white upon white in such a mad froufrou
as if these trees had never bloomed before
nor knew what unkind work east winds would do.

So brief this beauty one could almost cry,
for loveliest things are yet the saddest too;
each petal falls as gently as a sigh

since these are barren boughs that bear no berries.
I tell myself the months pass swiftly by.
Next April will bring back our flowering cherries.

Bliss is an Empty Room

Bliss is an empty room, a curtain glowing
yellow as sunlight, in the seawind blowing;
nothing else there
but a table, a chair,
a lamp to give light
and a bed for the night.

All now is done, all the to-ing and fro-ing,
all things sorted out for the selling or stowing,
all tidied and swept,
only special things kept,
things that we knew
would remind us of you.

Bliss is a quiet end and a joyful going
softly in sleep with the ebb tide gently flowing.
You would always maintain
those who love meet again.
Who am I to decry
a hope held so high?

Bliss is the harvest brought home, the reaping of sowing.
The promise has always been there but yet no foreknowing
that all will be well.
Time only will tell.
I will take things on trust –
for your sake I must.

Thyme in Sabratha

For Robin

This poem won't get itself written
    Tied up in a tangle of rhyme
Yet I remember Sabratha
    Whenever I season with thyme

For it grows in those Roman ruins
    Close to the ancient sea,
And I remember Sabratha
    Because you were there with me.

Too simple? A herb is simple
    And so is the cry of the heart.
You that were part of my being
    Are now a being apart.

Are you cold out there in the darkness?
    Or incandescent, refined
Into a loving spirit
    Part of the cosmic mind?

Wherever you are I shall find you
    Beyond these mortal bars
On that uncharted journey
    Out to the furthest stars,

So here's rosemary for remembrance,
    Rue for the herb of grace
And traveller's joy for my darling
    Gone to another place.

Low Days

What is this grey miasma, this chill mist,
This nothingness, this feeling of despair,
This dreadful deadweight of the leaden air,
This dark denial that will yet persist?
Death in the mind, the enemy within,
Numbness of heartstrings too inert to feel,
Dullness of eye, clamp on the feathered heel,
Annihilating every effort to begin
Once more, to face and stem the evil tide
That drowns the spirit in a sea of mud
And clogs the ardent courses of the blood.
For what remains when once the will has died
And all our little world is turned awry?
Nothing, a weary yawn, a hopeless sigh.

Rendezvous

Your chair still stands here halfway up the path
towards the terrace where the roses bloom
on the south wall; deserted, like your room,
your chair's now part of death's sad aftermath.

Here silence speaks, more eloquent than words;
here now the foxglove drooping in distress,
leans on the chairback in a half-caress
till twilight stills the calling of the birds

and halts the booming of the bumble bee
who loves to raid those rosy freckled flowers
and hum away the sleepy noontime hours
in concert with the far sound of the sea.

Here you would rest on the laborious trip
that brought you to the garden's upper reach
whence you might view the sea, the curving beach
and the white sail of some small sailing ship.

'How near he seems!' you said and caught your breath
and smiled as one who goes to meet her love,
serenely trusting in a God above
and that reunion promised after death.

December Legacy

Leave me your books; like you the year is dying.
The jasmine flowers, but I am desolate.
Black dawns, black days and sorrow at the gate,
Eyes all puffed up and red from too much crying.

Leave me your books, my loneliness forestalling,
So brave they stand like soldiers on their mark
To chase the paper tigers of the dark
And see off Death himself if he comes calling.

Leave me your books; you'll live between their covers
Now and for ever. What is time indeed?
You will be always with me as I read.
Leave me your books, last legacy of lovers

So I may find, as grief plays out his part,
The winter jasmine flowering in my heart.

ASTER GREENHILL

Lady Greenhill's granddaughter wrote this poem about ten years ago when she was ten or eleven. It is the only contribution from a 'diplomatic granddaughter' and has a charm of its own, making it well worth including in the anthology. Somewhat to her grandmother's surprise Aster has no objection to its publication!

I Wish

I wish I was an armadillo
I'd live in the desert with a rock as a pillow,
If a coyote comes near I roll up in a ball,
I am not such a tasty morsel after all.

I wish that I was a skunk,
I'd never need to get into a funk,
The strong-jawed fox would soon behave
Rather than try my aftershave.

I wish that I was a squid,
I would be in deep water whatever I did,
The sharks would have to have another think
When I blot myself out with ink.

I wish I was a family cat,
No habitat can be better than that.
If a human tries to stroke my head,
I stalk upstairs and glide under the bed.

PETER HINCHCLIFFE

I am now an academic, teaching and writing on Middle East politics – an area where I spent the bulk of my diplomatic life. I wrote a great amount of 'in-house' doggerel when serving as a Political Officer in the dying days of British rule in Aden and its Protectorates, mostly for the amusement (?) of my colleagues. I carried this habit into the Diplomatic Service but recently have written more serious stuff some of which has been published in poetry magazines. 'God! Am I Bored!', written when I was Ambassador in Jordan (and published in the diplomatic spouses' magazine), nearly got me into trouble with a humourless senior official who thought I was complaining about not having enough to do in Amman!

The Bag Lady's Revenge

O small dumpy figure. Dishevelled
and I suspect, unwashed. (Although
I have never gone down wind of you.)
Do people ever ask you what you
carry in your bag? Or don't they care?
Passing by carefully on the other side.
As I had, up to then.

Surely some sociologist could write
his thesis on the contents of your
plastic sack. (Why Sainsbury's, I wonder)
Perhaps one has. Got his doctorate
On the strength of it. Has no further use for you.
As I didn't, up to then.

So I stopped and asked you.
And although I do not entirely believe
all that you told me (especially about the small
tactical nuclear weapon). Still I am pleased
that I passed the time of day with you.
Which I hadn't up to then.

So if you carry out your promise
to castrate your two sons who have
ignored you all these years. And to reduce
Muswell Hill Broadway to mushroom clouded
oblivion, I will remember you with affection
and apologise (if I survive) for doubting all
you told me about the contents of your bag.
Which I do, up to now.

Christmas in Bethlehem

From the East the star arrived
Dead on time. As predicted.
More than can be said for the Three Wise Men.

One: ten days late.
(He had been following the wrong star.)
The other two had inadequate
documentation and were held up at the bridge.
Flowing robes arousing suspicion.
Gifts confiscated. Myrrh an illegal substance,
frankincense past its sell-by date,
and the rest thought to be probably stolen.

When they did arrive the star had long since left:
for Mecca, on another mission. There was no room
in any manger and all the cheaper inns were full.
Moreover no trace of their reservation at the King David Hotel.

Attempts to see the baby unsuccessful.
He could not be disturbed; his Press
Officer unavailable for comment.
Nor would Mary see them. 'Security reasons' they were told.
(Apparently there had been threats.)
The authorities were taking no chances.
So fed up and frustrated they took the first caravan home.

'Christmas in Bethlehem is much overrated'
they told their friends.

God! Am I Bored!

God! Am I bored!
Life is a doddle.
On top of my job.
Challenges gone.

What is the point
of being an Ambassador
when the country you serve in
is calm and peaceful? And they
all fall over themselves
to tell you what a marvellous
relationship exists
'between our two countries'.

I am bored out of my skull.
Not a problem in sight.
Day succeeds day:
hellishly predictable.

Oh! For a bit of excitement!
Not asking much. A small nuclear
device perhaps. Exploding
in parliament. Just loud enough
to wake some of the deputies
and to encourage the rest
into saying something. Anything.

It just happens that I have
such a thing (fell off the back
of an Iraqi lorry). Kept for
a rainy day, which we rarely have
in this tropical paradise.
So now is the moment to create
some thunder of my own.

I have made the necessary
arrangements. Tip off. Union Jack
on outer casing. So there can
be no mistaking
as to who was responsible
for this 'savage, unprincipled
and premeditated attack'.

And when the Foreign and Commonwealth
Office asks me why did I do it,
I will say I was bored out of my mind
and anxious to make an impact
on the bilateral relationship.
Which is the purpose of my mission.
And successful beyond expectations.

I will add that I am not bored.
Anymore.

The Ambassador

'Ambassador'. It has a certain ring.
Gravitas indeed. Demanding respect,
inviting deference. Rating a residence.
Not just a house. Commanding an embassy;
not a mere office. Nicely attired;
expensively too. Tie just right. Boring
on another man; but on an Ambassador:
distinguished. In excellent taste.
At least that is the perception.
And in diplomacy perception is all.
Form not substance. Mirage not reality.
The man is real enough. It is his message
which is flawed. A well dressed lie,
told by a well dressed liar. We admire
the singer and ignore the song.
The melody drowns the words.
We go on humming the tune
as we fall into the hole
the Ambassador dug for us.

And all that we remember
as we fall,
is what a nice man
he was.

The Unknown Country

Hard to remember. To close the car door
yourself. Should you have a car. If only a banger.
No patient friendly driver. Just the bus. Hopefully.
No obsequious official. No protocol greeter.
No one unctuously to ask His Excellency's health.
Smarmy, smiling. Cold eyes uncaring.

Freezing November. No climatic allowance.
The shabby Barbour will have to do another
winter. Inevitably the bus not materialising.
Splash out on a taxi. The cruising cabby. His eyes
in the rear mirror as calculating as any protocol officer,
pricing the overcoat. Sullenly resigned
to a meagre tip. No call for chat. Not worth the effort.

No management officer. No well ordered entitlements
befitting a hard earned status. You are your own
Personal Assistant. Gone, gone for ever
the smug security of a Residence. Smiling
considerate, unobtrusive servants. Clothes returned
ironed, immaculate.
(Now suffer the steamy laundrettes and the charity shop.)
And a well-stocked inventory: crystal and silver.
Try finding grape scissors in your local Safeways!

Out of the system. Well oiled security. Spat out at sixty.
A stranger in a community you thought you represented.
Rudderless in the reality of this modern Britain.
Retirement is an unknown country – a hardship posting.
Not on any list circulated by Personnel Department.
No competition for this assignment. Deserving
the hackneyed epithet, beloved of management:

'A Challenge'.
And I relish it.

NORMAN KELLY

Norman Kelly has contributed this poem inspired by a period of temporary duty in Havana in 1988. He retired from the Service in 1994, having served in various posts including the United States, Nigeria and Bulgaria. His last job was Consul in Helsinki.

Farewell to Havana

I will miss you, Old Havana;
No more to walk your graceful squares,
Nor find amongst your colonnades,
Shades of another bygone age.
And yet no dying city this,
For all around your old façade
A modern Cuba, full of life,
Throngs and dances through your streets.

I will miss you, Malecon;
No more to stroll your sunlit course,
As children skyward float their kites.
And anglers casting hopeful lines
Regard the surging sunlit surf.
Where sometimes in a trick of light,
There flits across Havana Bay
A spectral full-sailed ship in flight.

I will miss your vibrant echoes and your sights
San Cristobal de la Habana,
                              Adios

SIR HUGHE KNATCHBULL-HUGESSEN

I am indebted to Charles de Chassiron for sending me this unusual poem written by the late Hughe Knatchbull-Hugessen. Sir Hughe, a distinguished member of the Diplomatic Service between the two world wars, served as Envoy Extraordinary and Minister Plenipotentiary covering the three Legations at Riga, Tallinn and Kovno. But the Foreign Office regarded this appointment as one post and resourced it accordingly, to the incumbent's obvious disgust (not to mention impoverishment!). He later came to public attention, as the victim of the notorious spy Cicero, when Sir Hughe was ambassador to Turkey during the Second World War. His tenure of Riga etc. was obviously successful as he did not 'go to Bogota or La Paz everlastingly'. Given what happened at Ankara this may have been a pity!

Quicunque Balt

Whosoever will be saved, before all things it is necessary that he hold the Baltic Post.

Which post, except a man keep for a few years, without doubt he shall go to Bogota or La Paz everlastingly.

For the Baltic post is this, that we have one Minister in three capitals, and three capitals in one Minister.

Everyone confounding his person, and dividing his substance.

For there is one Minister for Lithuania, one Minister for Latvia and one Minister for Estonia.

But the Minister for Lithuania, for Latvia and for Estonia is all one; the uniform uncomfortable and the travelling almost eternal.

Such as Riga is, so is Tallinn and so is Kovno.

But Kovno in particular is uncreate and incomprehensible.

As also Riga is a Legation, Tallinn is a Legation and Kovno is a Legation.

And yet there are not three Legations but one Legation.

So also is Riga expensive, Tallinn is expensive and Kovno is expensive.

And yet there are not three salaries but one salary.

For like as we are compelled by the Private Secretaries to say there is one Legation and one Minister, so we are forbidden by the Chief Clerk[1] to say that there are three salaries or three frais de representation[2].

So likewise there should be one Secretary[3] for Riga, one Secretary for Tallinn and one Secretary for Kovno.

And yet there are not three Secretaries but no Secretary.

No Secretary, not by reduction of the Chancery[4] work into nothing, but by taking the Secretary to Moscow[5].

Absolutely none; by confusion of the Private Secretaries

And not by desire of the Minister.

The Minister is made and created and forgotten.

The Secretary is neither made nor created but proceeding to Moscow.

So there is one Minister, not three Ministers, one salary, not three salaries; no Secretary, not even one Secretary.

And in this Legation none is afore or after the other,

Although a good many people seem to be continually after the Minister.

The whole thing is most unequal and incomprehensible.

He therefore that would be saved, might sometimes think of HM Minister at Riga.

Such is the Baltic Post – although any reasonable soul will find it hard to believe faithfully.

---

1 A senior official overall responsible for the management of the Diplomatic Service.
2 An allowance payable to heads of missions to help cover the additional costs of mission of running an Embassy and residence.
3 A junior diplomat, as in 'Third Secretary'.
4 The political section of an Embassy.
5 Moscow was presumably the nearest fully-fledged Embassy and thus had a supervisory role with regard to Riga.

ELIZABETH PRICE

Diplomatic service is usually (but not certainly) in the ratio of three years in London to six years overseas. Home postings are not always eagerly sought after, for some of the reasons given in Elizabeth Price's poem which first appeared in print in 1986 in the Diplomatic Service's spouses' magazine. The other message is: one person's hardship post is another's paradise!

Lament on a Home Posting

When we went off to start our life
as British diplomats
to India's far shore we sailed
complete with gloves and hats.
A Hardship Post they told us,
this was going to be.
And so we braced ourselves to face
the problems willingly.

We soon got used to servants,
the heat and Monsoon rain.
And even Delhi Belly wasn't
too much of a pain.
The swimming pool, the tennis courts,
they catered for our leisure.
And India's rich heritage
gave many hours of pleasure.

While lounging by the swimming pool
sipping Nimbu Pani.
Someone said 'A Hardship Post,
the office must be barmy.
If this is hardship give us more
and we won't mind at all.
The fun of living overseas
beats problems large and small.'

For now as far as we're concerned
there's just one hardship post.
A transfer back to London
is the thing we fear the most.
A 10-hour day, no time for lunch,
weekend, night duty too.
And British Rail to cap it all;
it really will not do.

He does not mind a hard day's work,
the job he does enjoy.
But deserves just compensation
for the skills he does employ.
No spare cash, no social life,
the mortgage must be paid.
We feel we have missed the boat
unlike friends at home who stayed.

But we will grin and bear it
for some two years or three.
Until we hear the magic words
from dear old POD[1].
Then off we go to who knows where
to do our bit for Britain.
And I'll wonder why I felt so sad
when these few words were written!

---

1 Personnel Operations Department. Responsible for postings. Nice work if you can
get it.

SIR MARTIN REID

Martin Reid retired in 1988 after a career which took him to a variety of capitals including Rangoon, Paris, Georgetown, Bucharest and Lilongwe. His two most senior appointments overseas were Pretoria (as Minister) and High Commissioner, Kingston. He was also a Chairman of the Civil Service Selection Board. He is an artist whose paintings have been regularly exhibited. His poem will remind so many Foreign Service parents of the trauma of seeing off children back to school after a holiday at some remote post. Not to see them again for several months in many cases.

Chileka

The parting when it came,
came quickly.

We had spent the morning
packing and unpacking,
spinning out simple tasks
just to be doing something together.
Talking cheerfully about what we'd be
doing next holidays.
One last trip to the shops
and one last set of tennis before lunch.

When we saw the VC 10 come in to land
far away in the valley below
we set out without a word.

At Chileka there was pandemonium.
Passengers arriving and departing,
jostling with friends, relations, officials,
                    porters, baggage.

In all the hubbub
we just had time for a final goodbye
before they went through and were gone.

From up above we saw them later
walk out across the apron.
They turned and waved
knowing we would be there
but they did not see us.

We stood and watched the familiar departure
                    routines.
                    Eventually
they taxied heavily away and out of sight.

98

Then someone said 'Here they come'.
The VC 10 surged forward into view
and thundered past us down the runway.

Straining on full power
it lifted off;
tucked in its wheels
and banked away
setting course for Nairobi and Heathrow.

We watched until we could no longer see
the winking light on its underbelly.
Then we drove back up the hill
To a silent empty house.

CLARE ROGERS

Clare Rogers is the daughter of a recently retired member of the FCO. She is a social worker with an organisation in London which works to rehabilitate the mentally sick who are now 'in the community'.

My Father and My Father

I always hesitate outside the club
which is posh and really meant for men
of a certain status. I have to wear a skirt.

I wait in the lobby, not being
a member, and gaze at mounted shields
of public schools until you come.

Then, you arrive, and we're important.
I have access to a sherry in the lounge,
waiter service at table, and feel as though
by virtue of my dad, I too had made it in the FCO.

God once reminded me of this
and said, you did not know me,
you were not my child,
but now you are,
and everything I have is yours.

Nothing is barred, no door is closed,
no club too exclusive for you now;
come and find me in my secret rooms.
And: here is the love now for your father
you always had but couldn't say.

I've taken all the bars away.

PAULINE TAYLOR

Pauline Taylor's late husband Stan was a Security Officer in the FCO. Security officers are a distinct body of mostly ex-servicemen who are responsible for the physical security of our embassies. Sadly the corps is being phased out, as electronic surveillance becomes more efficient. After a well-travelled career the Taylors retired from Brussels in 1981 when Pauline's poem on retirement (evidently a popular theme in 'diplomatic verse') was published in the Diplomatic Service wives' magazine – in those days spouses were assumed to be female!

Retirement

Where did all the years go? Middle age came so fast.
They were good those years when I look back at the past.
A childhood that was full of fun.
Why do I only remember the sun?

The youngest one of seven girls
I watched them prink and tong their curls,
And I longed for the day when I would wear
An evening dress and do my hair,
And go to a ball or even a dance –
Alas I never got the chance.
The war took away my teenage years,
We razed the Hun but it brought its tears.

And when it was over and the few came back
This Wren married her jolly Jack.
And I thank the Lord for all the joys
That came to us with our three boys.
Between them they broke arms, legs and a skull,
And they certainly knew which heartstring to pull.

We've travelled the world the five of us.
We can pack and be gone without much fuss.
We've flown from Paris to Accra,
Sofia, Warsaw, Lusaka, Dakar.
The Foreign Office knows only too well
The places we've been – some heaven, some hell.
But for all our travels I couldn't forget
Our dear old England, cold, damp and wet.

We're grandparents now and how we are missing
Little girls growing up, their hugging and kissing.
I've longed to retire, but what can you do
With an active man who'd only be blue?
Then lo and behold we found some land
With a derelict house and we all thought it grand.

Only ten more months as a Dip. Service wife
Then to hell with diplomacy, we start 'The Good Life'.
When our house is ready I'll shout 'hip hooray'.
And tear up my passport – and home I'll stay.

TOM VAUGHAN

Tom Vaughan is the pen-name of a serving member of the Diplomatic Service currently working in London. One of his four poems, 'Abroad', has been previously published in the poetry journal Staple. *'Are You an English Gentleman?' neatly mocks the stiff upper lip image, which characterises the breed as viewed by many outside observers. See also Greg Dorey's 'The Tabloid Diplomat' elsewhere in this collection. 'Leaving Washington' is everyone's experience of moving on – this gets harder as you progress along your transitory career path leaving more and more friends behind you, with most of whom you inevitably lose touch.*

Abroad

I used to be jealous of friends
Who holidayed in Greece
Or Italy, but all
They brought back was a tan
And photographs of one another
In T-shirts, looking fat.
Behind there'd be
The Bridge of Sighs or the Aegean Sea.

And all they ever talked about was food –
Goat cheese, white peaches, cheap wine, the two ice cream
Shops in Florence
One mustn't miss
Where for the price of a McDonald's
Dark waiters serve
A procession of courses, a salad, plus a bombe;
Or how one had to live for weeks just like a peasant
Eating bread and olives on a beach.

I could learn more at an evening class.
Also, sometimes I think
It's who, not where you are which puts things
Out of reach.

Are You an English Gentleman?

Are you an English gentleman
Who always sees things through?
Are you an English gentleman
Regular and true?
Are you an English gentleman
Whose life of quiet despair
Seen from the outside, looks to be
Reliably square?
Are you part of the landscape
With a firm handshake
Understated savoir-faire?
Are you an English gentleman
Avoiding the public glare?

Are you an English gentleman
Unflappable under fire?
Annoyingly self-possessed,
Genetically a squire?

Are you an English gentleman
Never, never late?
Are you an English gentleman
Completely out of date?
Are you an English gentleman
Unable to cope
With foreign parts and feminists –
Have you become a joke?
Politically incorrect
An existential retrospect
A species under serious threat –
Are you an English gentleman
Bewildered but bespoke?

Are you an English gentleman
Although there's no such thing?
Are you an English gentleman
Whose timer has gone ping?
Are you an English gentleman?
If so, hang on old chap –
Let's dine out at my club tonight
And talk a load of crap.

Leaving Washington

We count the days. Thirty till we're
right out of here –
in twenty-one
the packers come –
lunches, dinners, saying farewell –
in parallel
more than enough
dull admin stuff
(accounts to close, phone bills to pay) –
no careless, stray
weekends to waste,
just pace, pace, pace. . .

Already in a way we've left
becoming deft
(in self-defence)
at shifting tense:
we live as if in retrospect,
to disconnect
(while shaking hands
and making plans)
from every brutal 'now'. You see,
time's alchemy
protects, transforms
(read, misinforms. . .) .

What we've done is accelerate
the standard rate
of forgetting,
imagining
time present as time past, a slick
internal trick
which gets us through
the ballyhoo.
It's useful practice anyway
against the day
we drop for good
all such deadwood.

Appropriate

Appropriate's a lovely word –
It doesn't mean a thing –
So useful when one needs a text
Appropriately thin –

'Appropriate measures may be used,
Appropriate forces sent' –
Appropriately you'll never know
Exactly what we meant

When unforeseen – of course – events
Raise the question why
Inappropriately innocent people
Die.

PETER VEREKER

Peter Vereker is Ambassador to the OECD in Paris, and was previously chairman of the Directing Staff at the Royal College of Defence Studies. A number of his poems have been published in The Times *and the* Literary Review, *and others, with musical settings by Beth Brown, wife of Sir Mervyn Brown, a former High Commissioner in Nigeria, have been performed in concert in London and Paris. His light-hearted 'Planners Lament' neatly satirises the post-cold war dilemma of identifying 'the threat'!*

Mosaic

Europe? Nothing to put your finger on.
A certain elegance of thought and line.
A willingness, its Age of Wars being gone
To mix some temperate water in the wine
Of sovereign power. An innovative kind
Of classical compulsion to excel,
With Christian merits, symmetries of mind,
And courtesies which suit their bearers well.
No nothing firm, a richness in the air,
Awareness of new links that will not break,
And reverence for what was always there
The many-sided charm of the mosaic.
　　　So we should all, as part of this, be proud
　　　To say we're Europeans clear and loud.

Barricades

The curtain lifts, the iron in the soul
Was suddenly consigned to memory.
The fate that Marx and Lenin once foresaw
Befell their own discarded theory.
Yet other barriers have still remained
Twixt those who feel and those who would be free
Free from self-doubt or penury or pain
Which barricade the road to liberty.
And there are walls to climb within ourselves
Which neither tanks nor politics may breach.
Each our own course of mental obstacles
Before we shall our liberation reach.
　　　The lights have come back on. Now let them shine
　　　Upon those lives set free and yours and mine.

113

Rearguard

Outside the still and shadowed room
The rhododendrons are in bloom
And sunlight glances on the leaves

It shimmers on the windowpane
The pony clopping down the lane
The raindrops falling from the eaves

A breeze has chased the clouds away
But having come equipped to stay
Their rearguard lingers on the hill

So, far off in Afghanistan,
A like retreating caravan
Has ceased at last to cow and kill.

The gusts are swirling here and there
Who knows when clouds may reappear
But we have reason to be glad

While they must miss in soul and mind
The fifteen thousand left behind
And no advantage to be had

We could have told them had they wished
For English armies too perished
In hills beyond Jalalabad

The pony's fading hoofbeats sound
Resembling on the drying ground
A fusillade of distant fire

Close by, safe from an Afghan gun,
A nightingale, cheered by the sun,
Sings like a minstrel choir.

Planners Lament

When God was in *our* heaven
The devils knew their place
But now the Old Religion
Has lost that interface.

Then we were part of NATO
And They the Warsaw Pact
But now we only Wait-oh
When others attacked.

We liked the Old Religion
It kept us safe you see
And gave us the protection
Of Bipolarity.

If Ministers so order
We'll still go off to fight
But life was so much simpler
When Black was never White.

Now Russians are our allies
And we're in blue berets
We don't know what The Threat is
Come back - Dear Enemies!

When *we* did the arranging
The Devils knew the score
Now all the tunes are changing
And Planners sing no more.

WINEFRED WHITE

Winefred White retired from the Diplomatic Service in July 1981. Her last post was Nairobi, which she must have enjoyed as she still lives in Kenya. Her poem 'HM Consul – On Retirement' she recited at her farewell party and it will strike an immediate chord with anyone who has had a consular job overseas, especially in those countries where the demand for UK visas seems insatiable and where visiting Brits do not always behave impeccably and expect immediate service from the local diplomatic mission.

HM Consul – on Retirement

No more shall I issue an emergency
        passport
At nine o'clock on a Saturday night.
Says the Security Officer: 'The lady's
        quite distraught,
Her handbag's been stolen. She must catch
        her flight.'

No more calls from Patel. 'Please
        give me a visa
To go to London, I'm booked on the
        plane.
I must see my brother, he's had a
        seizure.'
I ask 'Are you planning to come back again?'

No more at four on a Friday, the week's nearly
        over.
Here come two hippies. They look
        stoned on hash.
I say 'Social Security ends at Dover.
You must ring up your Mum if you've
        run out of cash.'

No more dear old ladies who've gone
        a bit gaga,
Now that I have hung up my
        consular hat.
No more angry travellers whose plane
        won't go further.
It's July 24th – and goodbye to all
        that.

118

THE COLLEAGUES

As a tailpiece I am including a poignant little poem written by the wife of a former Portuguese Ambassador to Bulgaria in 1984. Jennifer Snodgrass, whose husband was at the time British Ambassador in Sofia, sent it to Diplomatic Service Spouses' Association for publication in their magazine.

Ambassador's Wife's Lament

This life of mine
made of arrivals and departures
where the first meeting
is the beginning of a parting
– poor shaking-waving hands.

This destiny of mine
mysteriously attached to some sailing ship
pressingly awaiting me wherever I go.

And my memories
which I must carry on my shoulders
in my heart.

So used to partings . . .
One day I will part for ever,
and I'll think it's for a new assignment.
And it will be so, indeed:

A post where
God will be the Head of Mission.

'Come and rest, you poor traveller'
I'll look at Him
– oh that merciful face!
I'll throw away my cases,
my old passport.

'May I bring my memories with me?'
'They are already waiting for you.'
Step by step
I'll come to the everlasting meeting.

'Don't forget to take off your sandals.
You won't need them anymore.'
And my poor errant life
will finish in his arms.

ODDS AND ENDS

In especially the remoter posts the importance of home mail and supplies of essentials getting through looms large in people's lives. JUDY RAPP's *contribution about a long-delayed order from a British company specialising in sending goods to far-flung places not quite reaching its anxious customers at an unnamed Commonwealth capital has an authentic ring and reminds me vividly of life in Tanzania in the late 1970s. As does the anonymous 'Bagless's Christmas Lament' written in Khartoum in 1976 and sent in by* STELLA CRAVEN, *who feels that it sums up a posting which some people regarded as 'the end of the line'. The non-arrival of the 'bag' bringing letters and parcels from home, especially at a time like Christmas, could seem like a major disaster.*

Diplomatic Spouses' Association Tea

Women sit, chat, sip,
eating cake.
The Chairwoman speaks –
'Any notices?'
A voice is heard:
'the Food will be
here
on Friday'.
Scattered applause.
We've heard that one
before.
The vultures in the tree
look in
and grin.

Bagless's Christmas Lament

(With apologies to A.A. Milne)

Khartoum is not a bad place:
It has its lows and peaks;
And sometimes no one writes to us
For weeks and weeks and weeks.
And round about December
The cards upon our shelves
Are never from our near and dear
But only from ourselves.

Khartoum is not a bad place:
It lives up to our fears.
We have received no presents now
For years and years and years.
And every year at Christmas
The staff all weep and moan;
They search the starry skies in vain
For any inkling of a plane:
But British Air say, once again
That they have overflown.

Khartoum is not a bad place
We live our lives aloof .
Alone we thought a telex out
Whilst sunning on the roof.
We sent it top priority
(and hoped there'd be no slips)
'To all and sundry, near and far,
the Bag room[1] in particular –
it would be quicker far by motor car
or Camel Train – Phillips[2.]

'I want some of my bags
right here – in Khartoum.
We've got COI bags[3]
Stacked up in every room.
I don't mind what flight they come
Any one will do:
Lufthansa, Aeroflot
(but not to Katmandu[4])
And, Oh! David Pugh[5]: if you love us at all
Please post our Christmas presents
Next year – before the Fall.'

---

1 Bag room: FCO section responsible for mail.
2 Telexes always went out under the surname of the Ambassador.
3 Official Publicity (propaganda!) material from the Central Office of Information (COI). No substitute for personal mail – often seemed to get through when private mail didn't.
4 Posts whose names began with the same letter occasionally got the other posts' mail – especially at busy times like Christmas.
5 I suspect he was the head of the Bag room!

A LIMERICK

In-house poetry often as the result of an informal competition in say, an embassy, is quite common within the FCO. When Sir Sam Falle was about to leave Stockholm at the end of his stint as Ambassador in 1977 he sent in his valedictory despatch (end of assignment report to the Foreign Secretary) entitled 'Farewell to Paradise'. Members of the Embassy and of the FCO department dealing with Sweden organised a limerick competition to mark Sam Falle's departure. The winner was FRANCIS RICHARDS, *then of Western European Department, whose effort is below. I am indebted to the Hon. Ivor Lucas — ex-FCO — for drawing it to my attention. Sam Falle continues to reside in what he obviously still regards as Paradise.*

Theologians have never agreed on
The site of the Garden of Eden:
      But there is no doubt at all
      That the scene of the Falle
Has been rediscovered in Sweden.

AND FINALLY AN ODE

My final example of in-house verse is, I fear, my earliest attempt to let off some steam in this way during my first months in the FCO. I was in a very overstretched department – Near Eastern Department (NED) – containing fortunately some of my brightest contemporaries including a former Head of the Diplomatic Service, Sir Anthony Acland, Veronica Sutherland – now Ambassador to Ireland – and Christopher Long – just retired as Ambassador to Hungary – for whose amusement the ditty was written. E—s, I can now reveal, is Sir Richard Evans, who retired as Ambassador to Peking some years ago. In 1969 he was the Assistant Head of NED. A meticulous man, he insisted on the highest standards of drafting and presentation. We juniors working to very tight deadlines (sometimes late into the night) never really got used to our work being sent back for revision for what we regarded as unnecessary attention to trivial detail. In the pre-word processor era revision, in effect, meant starting again.

Ode from a Fan

E—s was a pedant with a brain as clear as grass.
When drafts came through to him he'd never let them pass,
without a gentle sigh, a softly murmured 'quite'.
Then – 'Not too bad considering, but the flavour isn't right.'

'Presentation is what matters whenever you submit
be it to the Private Secretary or to some other languid twit.
Substance? Well it matters; but its importance is so slight
when compared to the necessity of the flavour being right.'

E—s then would cogitate for simply hours on end,
redrafting and redrafting 'til he drove us round the bend.
The point of the submission[1] was finally lost to sight;
but 'Ah! Ce ne fait rien [2] when the flavour will be right.'

Enfin we could not stand it; it was either us or him,
so we filled his cup of coffee with arsenic to the brim.
E—s softly murmured as with death he lost the fight:
'The coffee is unimpressive but they've got the flavour right.'

---

1 A submission is a document proposing a course of action – usually to a Minister.
2 The convention was that foreign language phrases should be underlined. A practice
which Dr David Owen on becoming Secretary of State attempted to stop.